Instagram: Insider Tips and Secrets on How to Gain Followers and Likes that Work Fast

by Neo Monefa

THANK YOU FOR DOWNLOADING! IF YOU WOULD LIKE TO BECOME APART OF OUR READER COMMUNITY AND RECEIVE UPDATES ON UPCOMING TITLES PLEASE EMAIL PARAMOUNTPUBLISHINGCOMPANY@GMAIL.COM

Table of Contents

1. Introduction

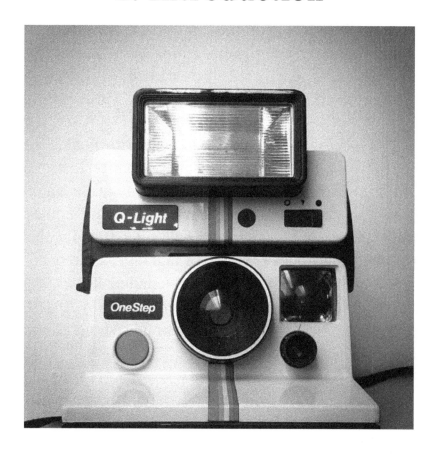

Even if you don't use Instagram, we're guessing you've encountered an Instagram image somewhere on the web — even if you didn't realize it.
Instagram's calling card is the photo filter, a digital layer that, when added to a standard photo, gives it the appearance of professional editing. Some filters enhance the colors in a photo, while other dull the light to a soft glow for an aged, vintage appearance.

But while Instagram's filters revolutionized mobile photo editing, they're only a portion of the appeal. The mobile app boasts over 50 million users, despite only living in iOS and Android devices. Instagram launched on Android just this year — it quickly earned 5 million downloads in six days.

Its success caught the eye of the most valuable social network in the world. Facebook acquired Instagram in April for $1 billion. Although we've only just begun to witness Facebook's plans for the photo sharing app, the social giant recently launched its own filter-friendly photo app, dubbed Facebook Camera. Instagram has surely come a long way, business-wise, since co-founders Kevin Systrom and Mike Krieger introduced the app in 2010. But on the whole, the app has remained simple, straightforward and social since its inception.

A popular mobile photo and video sharing social networking site, Instagram isn't only for the casual user who merely wants to share their posts with their family. Instagram is a powerful tool for people who utilize it correctly. And businesses of all sizes have seen the benefits that Instagram provides. Businesses and companies who use Instagram correctly have seen an increase in sales and leads just by actively engaging others on the site. It is no wonder that celebrities and people in the public eye use Instagram to get their message across and connect with fans.
But you don't have to be rich and famous to get the most out of your Instagram account. This book will not only

show you how to properly use Instagram, but it also provides you with insider tips that are proven to gain followers and likes fast. So what are you waiting for? Get started in the wonderful world of Instagram today!

2. The Skinny on Instagram

Breaking out on the scene in 2010, Instagram is a fairly new social media networking that utilizes the popularity of smartphones and their capabilities to snap photos. Essentially, Instagram is a mobile app that lets you to snap, edit and share photos all with your smartphone. The app includes various filters that you can use on your photos to alter their look. For example, one filter can give your photo a professional glow while another filter gives it an old school Polaroid look. In 2012, the monster social media site Facebook purchased Instagram for $1 billion in stock and cash. And even though it was hugely popular beforehand, the Facebook connection only intensified the popularity of Instagram.

Just to show you how popular Instagram is, there are an estimated 60 million photos uploaded to the app every day. That's around 700 photos are uploaded every second.

So with that many photos being added to Instagram every day, how are you supposed to stand out and get followers and likes? The info in this book will show you how.

3. Getting Started: How to Create and Use your Instagram Account

Instagram is relatively easy to setup and use. Before you can reap the benefits of Instagram, however, you must first create an account, which means you have to download the app to your smart phone. You can get the app from the Apple App Store (for iPhones) or the Google Play Store (for Androids).

Once you have the app downloaded, tap on the Instagram icon to launch the app. Next, tap the word "Register" and begin filling out the required information. Once you have completed the registration, you have the option to important you friends and contacts from your Twitter account, Facebook account and/or your phone's contact list. If you would rather not connect them at the moment, you will still be able to do so in the future if you so desire. Furthermore, you can search Instagram for usernames and names and add your friends at any time.

After registering, a "follow suggested users" screen will pop up. This is just some random users that Instagram thinks you might be interested in. If you want to follow them, simply click the "Follow" bottom by their name. This isn't a requirement and you can skip this step by simply clicking on the "Done" button.

Your profile shows your bio and the photos and videos you've posted to Instagram. From your profile, you can also edit your profile information and adjust your Account Settings. You can navigate to your profile by tapping the person icon in the toolbar at the bottom of the screen, and make changes by tapping the "Edit Your Profile" button or access more information and choices by tapping the gear icon to access Options. You can write a bio of up to 150 characters on your profile, or add or change a profile photo to import from your phone's library, Facebook, or Twitter. Also from your profile, you can access your Photo Map, which enables you to showcase where you've taken the photos you've shared.

The camera enables you to take photos with the Instagram camera or share photos from your phone's photo library. You can access the camera by tapping the center icon in the toolbar at the bottom of the screen, and from there can take a photo or video or choose a photo from your photo library.

You can use the Search & Explore function to find people to follow, search for specific users, and explore hashtags. Access Search & Explore by tapping the magnifying glass icon in the toolbar at the bottom of the screen, and toggling between the "Photos" and "People" views to explore posts and users, or type in the "Search" box and choose between "Users" and "Hashtags."

The Home tab shows the feed of photos posted by you and by the other Instagram users whom you follow. You can like and comment on the photos and videos in your Feed. Access your feed by tapping the Home button in the toolbar at the bottom of the screen.

The Activity tab displays likes and comments on your posts, and shows you the photos and videos that your friends are liking and commenting on. You can access the Activity tab by tapping the speech bubble icon in the toolbar at the bottom of the screen, and toggling between the "Following" and "You" views.

4. Taking Photos

Before you start snapping away, you should know that all photos and videos uploaded to Instagram have a default privacy setting of public. This means that anyone using the app or the Instagram website can see your photos and videos. You can, however, change this setting and make your photos and videos private by simply changing the privacy setting on your account to private. What this does is limit whom can see your media to only your followers.

Instagram allows you to either take a photo directly from the app or upload an existing photo in your phone's camera roll. No matter which way you use, you will need to click the camera tab located in the center of the app's navigation panel. This activates the camera. If you want to take a photo, simply click the large tab in the center. For video, click the video recorder tab. If, however, you want to use a picture or video saved on your phone, tap the square button found at the bottom of your screen. This will bring up all your photos and videos saved on your phone.

After you have taken or selected your photo, you can then edit it by rotating the image, cropping it or use one of the many filters available on the app.

When you're ready to post your photo or video, simply tap the next button. A screen will appear that allows you to type a description of your media. This is where you will also add hashtags, which help people locate your photo.

More than a platform for users to post photos of expensive lattes — often complete with edits and filters applied with a heavy hand — Instagram is becoming an increasingly popular and powerful social network. The Facebook-owned photo sharing app is still significantly smaller than Facebook, the most ubiquitous social network in the world. But Instagram is growing much more quickly than Facebook, as new users like you join every day to connect not only with their friends, but with a global community of users who share photos and videos from their everyday lives on the platform.

When you first download Instagram, it's apparent that the app has a lot of features, and it's not always obvious to a new user how to navigate Instagram or how to get started. So we've made you a beginner's guide to Instagram, one that will point you in the right direction and show you everything you need to know, from how to set up your account and how to find people to follow to how to post a photo or a video or how to use Photo Maps, Instagram Direct, or even how to use Instagram on the web.

The camera enables you to take photos with the Instagram camera or share photos from your phone's photo library. You can access the camera by tapping the center icon in the toolbar at the bottom of the screen, and from there can take a photo or video or choose a photo from your photo library.

Once you've chosen a photo, you can add effects from the editing tools at the top of the screen or select a filter from the choices at the bottom of the screen. Then you can write a caption for the photo, tag people in the photo, add it to your Photo Map, or share it to Facebook, Twitter, Tumblr, or Flickr. When you write the caption to your photo, you can use hashtags and mentions. Mentions let you bring a post to the attention of another user — who will get a notification when you mention him or her in a post — and hashtags will help other Instagram users to find your posts, or help you to tag or categorize your posts for yourself.

To tag people in a photo, tap "Tag People" and tap on someone in the photo. Start entering their name or username, and select the correct users from the dropdown menu that appears. If the person that you want to tag doesn't appear in that menu, tap "Search for a person" to find him or her. If your photos are public, then anyone can see the photo, and the person tagged in the photo will get a notification. If your photos are private, then only people who are following you will be able to see the photo. The person whom you tag in the photo will get a notification if they're following you. (You can see and manage the photos that other people tag you in from your profile.)

When you post your photo, it will appear both on your profile and in your feed. If you've set your profile to private, only the people whom you've approved to follow you will be able to see it.
Below the description will be various share options, such as Facebook, Twitter, Tumblr and Flickr. When you select

one or more of these options, your photo or video as well as the description will automatically post to the selected social media network. Keep in mind, however, that you will need to connect your account from those other social media networks to your Instagram in order for the sharing option to work properly.

When you are ready to share, tap the "Share" bottom. And voilà! Your photo or video is posted to your Instagram account, as well as any other accounts you selected to share it to.

5. The Tab Layout

Once you are registered and logged in to the Instagram app, you will see 5 tabs or icons along the bottom of the screen. This is called the navigation panel. Remember that the Apple and Android versions of the Instagram app look different from one another, but will operate in the same manner.

- Feed Tab (Home/House Icon) – Clicking on this tab takes you to your feed. It is similar to how the Facebook feed works. It allows you to scroll through – in real time – the posts uploaded by the users you follow.
- Search Tab (Magnifying Glass Icon) - You can search the photos or people on Instagram by using usernames or hashtags.
- Share Tab (Camera Icon) – This is the tab you click on to either take a photo or video or select one from your phone to share on Instagram.
- Activity Tab (Thought/Speech Bubble Icon) – Clicking this tab shows you the updates or activity of the people you are following as well as the activity on your account. For example, when someone likes or comments on one of your posts or starts following you, it will show on this page.
- Account Tab (Person Icon) – If you want to view your Instagram profile or change any of the settings, click the account tab.

6. Not Just for Photos: Instagram's Video Feature

As detailed in the chapter above, Instagram has a video feature that allows you to post short 15-second clips. This feature wasn't available when the app first launched. In fact, the video feature didn't become available until the spring/summer of 2013.

Using Instagram's video feature is extremely similar to sharing a photo. Simply click on the share/camera tab located in the middle of your navigation panel. Then click on the video recorder tab to switch from camera mode to video mode. From here you can either record a new video or use a previously recorded video on your phone.

When recording a new video, you have the option of recording one continuous shot or multiple video segments. Both options have a maximum video time of 15-seconds.

Once you are ready to start recording, press and hold the large video recorder icon. Once you lift your finger off the button, the video will stop recording. When you want to start recording again, simply press and hold the video icon again. Click the "Next" tab to continue. You can now add a filter and/or edit the video.

When ready, tap the "Next" button, which takes you to the description and share page. Just as when you are sharing photos, this page allows you to add a description and cross post the video to your other social networking profiles. When ready, click the "Share" tab to upload the video.

7. Using Instagram's Direct Message Feature

At one time, any photo or video uploaded to Instagram was added to your account, which means everyone (if your account was public) or at the very least, your followers (if your account was private) were able to see them. It wasn't until late 2013 that Instagram added a direct message feature – also known as DM – to their app. The direct message feature gives you the ability to send a photo or video directly to another Instagram user. And the only one able to see the media is the users you choose.

There are two methods to sending a direct message: selecting a certain user at the share screen or through the inbox. When you upload a new photo or video to Instagram, there is an option to submit/send the media to your Followers or Direct. The default setting for this option is Followers. However, you can simply tap the Direct tab to send the image or video to only certain user(s). When you click on the "Direct" tab, Instagram will show you a list of suggested users that you regularly interact with. You can either scroll down the list to find the correct person or type the specific person's username in the search field. When ready to share, just click the "Send to" tab.

The second option to sending a direct message on Instagram is through your message inbox, which is the inbox-shaped icon located on your home/feed screen. Clicking on this icon will take you to your inbox where you can see all the direct messages you have sent and received. At the top of the screen with be a + icon. Clicking this icon takes you to the camera/video screen where you go through the same taking/recording/choosing, editing and uploading process of the image or video. In this case, however, the default setting is Direct.

8. Gaining Followers and Getting Likes: Steps that will Increase the Amount of Followers your Instagram Account Has and How Many Likes you Receive

You should construct a plan of action that focuses on posting quality content and maximizing your follower engagement before chugging full steam ahead. Having a game plan beforehand helps to improve your chance of success on this popular social media network. Keep the following insider tips in mind when creating your plan of action.

Fill Out your Profile
Most users will click on someone's profile before the decide whether or not to follow. If, however, your profile isn't complete, it could be turning away potential followers. That is why it is important to add a profile picture and description. You should also add a link to your website if you have one.

Connect your Facebook Account
Connecting your Facebook account to your Instagram account lets your Facebook friends easily find and follow you on Instagram.

Follow Others

Most all social media formats have an unwritten rule of reciprocation. That doesn't mean you have to follow someone simply because they are following you, but most users do return the favor. To find users to follow, search for brands and users that have the same interest as you. Then simply follow, comment and like. In other words, engage them and be active. The truth is, the more active and engaging you are on Instagram, the more exposure you will get.

Utilize Hashtags

Hashtags are essentially a word or group of words that follow the hashtag – or pound – symbol. When you add them to the description of your Instagram images and videos, it creates a link that – when clicked on – shows you other images and videos tagged with that same word or words.

You can use hashtags that have been already used or make up your own. Many businesses create their own brand hashtags and encourage their followers to use it. KitKat, for example, encourages their followers to use the #haveabreak hashtag across multiple social media accounts (Instagram, Facebook, Twitter and Google+).

If you are at a loss as to what hashtag to use, consider using hashtags that are currently trending. Trending hashtags are the ones being used the most at a given moment. Unlike other social media networks, Instagram doesn't currently provide users with which hashtags are trending. However, there are several websites that allow you to view the top hashtags trending on Instagram at the very moment.

Keep in mind, however, that you should try to only use hashtags that fit the image or video. For example, if you take a picture of your cat, use hashtags like #cats, #cat, #feline, #catsofinstagram, #kitty, and #kittycat. You can also add descriptive hashtags. For example, if your cat is black, add the hashtag #blackcat. Just keep it relevant to the image/video. You wouldn't want to tag a picture of your cat with the #dog hashtag now would you?

Like Other's Photos and Videos

Liking images and videos is the most common way that users on Instagram interact with one another. Simply liking the images of people you don't already follow can drive them to your profile. And if they like what they see, they will follow your account.

Comment and Comment a Lot

Commenting on other's photos is a great way to engage Instagram users and increase the amount of followers you have. Commenting on other's media is more personal than simply liking their photos/videos. You can either keep the comment simple – such as "love this!" – or more detailed, like "Your hair looks amazing! I wish I could get mine to look that good."

Post Regularly But Don't Over Do It

Regular posting is vital to gain followers. However, you shouldn't over do it. Posting too many images can turn people away and even result in a loss of followers. Most social media experts recommend posting between 1 to 10 photos or videos a day. Furthermore, make sure to space the photos out during the day. Remember, you are trying to engage users by ensuring one of your images or videos are always on their feed.

Get Shoutouts

A shoutout is essentially a call to action that tells users to go follow a certain person. For example, an Instagram page for people who have beards will tell its users to DM (Direct Message) them a picture. The beard page will then upload the picture to their Instagram account and give a shoutout to that user. This can lead to an increase in followers. To get shoutouts, simply follow an account that has an abundance of followers and regularly gives shoutouts. You can also search the #shoutout hashtag to find accounts.

Upload Only Quality Photos

You should always be concerned with quality when you are adding images and videos to your Instagram account. Uploading blurry, out of focus and boring photos will drive people away from your profile. Take a look at your own Instagram feed. Do your photos bore you? If they do, then I can ensure you they are also boring your potential followers.

Choose a Niche

It is no secret that some of the most popular Instagram accounts are ones that have a theme. What does this mean exactly? Well, the extremely popular Grumpy Cat has her own Instagram account where she regularly posts photos and videos of herself as well as other felines. That is her theme or niche. Another example is a popular Target sales account that posts the latest deals and savings from the department store Target. Now that doesn't mean you have to post images and videos that only fit into your theme. Just try to keep the majority of your content related to your niche.

Interact With Your Followers

You cannot simply gain followers and likes and then not engage the users. This will cause you to lose your fan base. That doesn't mean you have to respond to every single comment or like you receive, but you should at least try to regularly return the favor. Furthermore, if a follower asks you a question in the comment section, you should try your best to answer them. This will not only help keep the followers you already have, but will also show potential followers that you engage and respond to them.
Using a free website like IconoSquare lets you easily like, comment and respond all from the comfort of your computer. This can make the engaging process a bit faster than if you typed it all out on your smart phone. Furthermore, IconoSquare provides you with statistics about how well your images and videos are performing.

Ask Questions

Asking a question in the caption/description is a great way to get followers and nonfollowers engaged. It will also increase the amount of likes you receive on that photo/video. For example, if you post a photo of your Starbucks latte, ask your followers which is their favorite drink at Starbucks or what they would recommend the next time you visit the coffee shop.

Add your Instagram Feed to your Website

Adding your Instagram feed to your website can entice visitors to your site to your Instagram profile, where they can become a follower. This will only work if you have a website, such as a blog, portfolio or business site. If you don't currently have a website but are interested in creating one, you can use free platforms, such as Wordpress.com or Blogger.com.

Join Follow for Follow or Like for Like Groups

There are several groups on Facebook designed to increase the amount of followers or likes an Instagram account has. In these groups, you simple post a link to your Instagram profile or a link to a certain post and comment with "Follow for Follow" or "Like for Like". The people in the group will then follow you or like your photo. Just remember that you must return the favor.

Buy Followers

Buying Instagram followers can increase the amount of followers you have in a short amount of time with little to no work on your part. The amount of new followers you get will depend on the business and the package you choose. The more followers you want the more you will have to spend. Keep in mind, however, that the whole buying followers is a bit controversial with many people thinking it is wrong and shady practice, especially for businesses and people in the public eye.

Host Contests

If you want to gain new followers and boost engagement, hold a contest on your Instagram account. This is a proven tactic on just about all social networking sites. Creating a contest is easy and can be up and running in a matter of minutes. Simply take a great picture – preferably one that shows what the contest is for or what they will win – and then inform users in the caption/description that you are holding a contest. Don't forget to use the hashtag #contest and share the posts on your other social networking sites, such as Facebook, Twitter, Pinterest and Google+.

9. Other Apps that Work Great with Instagram

The following is a list of free and paid apps that pair well with Instagram. Some of the apps are available on both iPhone and Android smart phones, while others are not.

Pic Stitch

When one photo isn't enough, you can create a collage using this free app, available on both Android and iPhone devices. Pic Stitch offers many basic layouts, as well as some more advanced ones. There are also some layouts that will require purchasing within the app to use.

Aviary

Aviary is a full-on mobile photo editor that gives you the ability to fully edit your photos. Cropping, lighting, color, sharpness, blemish, focus, blur, vignette, whiten and redeye are just a few of the controls available on this free app. Aviary also has several filters, stickers, frames and other effects you can add to your photos. There are some additional filters and other effects that will require in app purchase to use.

Snapseed

This free photo-editing app is popular with creative types and bloggers. It provides control over almost every aspect of your photos. From small adjustments to auto correct, Snapseed has you covered.

Overgram

This nifty free app lets you add text right on your photos. You can choose from various fonts and text colors, and have complete control over where to position the text.

Slow Shutter Cam

Smart phone cameras are great in many ways but don't have the ability to take photos with a long-exposure. The Slow Shutter Cam app, however, has fixed that problem. This paid app gives you the ability to lengthen the shutter speed on iPhones. The app also has a Manual and Automatic capture mode.

10. Instagram for Business Marketing

If you create a company Instagram account and if you have other social media accounts, you can publish your photos on Twitter, Facebook, Flickr, Tumblr, Posterous, and Foursquare, or send them to email addresses. Instagram users can choose to "follow" your company account. They will see your photos in their feed and it allows them to "like," comment on, or Retweet your company's photos, allowing them to go viral. There are a lot of outdoor ads that promote Instagram accounts of companies in order to raise the number of followers on Instagram. Example, they can place a billboard with a photo from Instagram and write below: "click on an image to view information about the new Instagram Contest on an Instagram page".

Instagram for Business: How Does It Differ From Other Image Blogs?

You can add filters to their photos – this is the unique feature among others. You can create a specific color, shade, and look for your photos to match the message or mood that you want your audience to sense. Don't limit yourself on the types of images that you post; be creative and show the connection between the image and your brand.

Put Your Business on the Map
You can find your fans on Instagram in such a way; Instagram users may already be posting images related to your brand. Just go to your Instagram app and tap "Profile" in the menu at the bottom of your screen. Tap "Search Instagram" and then "Tags". Type in the name of your company/brand and let the images load. You can Retweet these images to enhance the community feeling around your brand. Make sure to geotag your photos. In other words, make sure to note where your photos were taken before uploading them to your account. Your company's location on the map is another valuable entry point for potential followers. Your Instagram account is also viewable on the web on Webstagram. Users can browse your photos on their computers, and not just their mobile devices. Instagram for business is only growing; start capturing more mindshare today with this fun and fairly simple set-up.

11. Instagram + Content

Creating content on Instagram Content is central to the Instagram experience. It's why tens of millions of people visit the app every day--to view beautiful, interesting imagery in their feed and to post their own unique photos and videos. The sharing of this visual art is what makes the Instagram community so dynamic and engaged. Your brand's content should add to the experience of being on Instagram for your followers. We recommend the following guidelines for creating content on Instagram:

1. Identity & voice: Develop a framework for bringing your brand's identity to life on Instagram, based on your business objectives. Identify words that reflect your brand's voice and tone; the feelings you want followers to associate with your brand; and the role you want your brand to play in their lives. This framework will inform your content, and in turn the experience that followers have when viewing your images.

2. Content themes: Establish regular content themes, or pillars, that are authentic to your brand and fit the Instagram platform. Ensure that your posts adhere to these pillars. This allows for a diversity of content that also remains consistent over time. Followers will know what to expect from your brand on Instagram as you reinforce key brand associations.

3. Image subjects: Post photos and videos of unexpected and behindthe-scenes moments that feel authentic and immediate. Candid, insider access is what people love about Instagram. We recommend avoiding overly promotional images or those that are simply repurposed from other channels. These images appear out of place on the platform and detract from establishing a clear and differentiated brand identity and voice.

4. Image enhancement: Adjust your images with filters and other tools available through the Instagram app.

These effects give images that unmistakable "Instagram" look that people respond to.

5. Text: Keep captions short and fresh. Incorporate hashtags where relevant, but not so many that they detract from the simplicity of the post. (Refer to section on hashtags for more guidance). Ask questions in the captions of your images to engage with followers

6. Location & people: Include the location of your photo or video when it helps tell the story of the image (i.e. it was taken at an event, roadshow, retail location, company headquarters). Use the Add People feature to tag accounts in your image when they will help you reach a broader audience and you have permission (i.e. partner brands, celebrity spokespeople, etc.)

7. Timing: Moderate the number of posts you make per day to ensure a consistent but non-intrusive presence. We recommend anywhere from 1-3 posts per day. Experiment with posting at different times of day by monitoring engagement. If posting content from a live event, consider creating a separate account to avoid annoying your followers by taking over their feeds

Conclusion

Instagram is a fun and engaging social media network that is like no other. It does take time and work to increase your followers into the thousands. However, if you use the methods discussed in this book, you will get the most out of your Instagram account and gain more followers and likes.

Thank You so much for reading this book. If this title gave you a ton of value, It would be amazing for you to leave a REVIEW !

THANK YOU FOR DOWNLOADING! IF YOU WOULD LIKE TO BECOME APART OF OUR READER COMMUNITY AND RECEIVE UPDATES ON UPCOMING TITLES PLEASE EMAIL PARAMOUNTPUBLISHINGCOM PANY@GMAIL.COM

www.ingramcontent.com/pod-product-compliance
Lightning Source LLC
Chambersburg PA
CBHW051218050326
40689CB00008B/1354